THE ROYAL BOOK OF BALLET

By

Shirley Goulden

Illustrated by

Maraja

Follett Publishing Company

CHICAGO NEW YORK

PRINTED IN ITALY
Fratelli Fabbri Editori - Milano

Library of Congress Catalog Card Number: 64-16319

SBN   695-50040-6   Titan binding
SBN   695-90040-4   Trade binding
THIRD PRINTING

At the ballet, chatter and movement around us subside. The light dims and then brightens on stage to reveal another world, peopled by darting, graceful forms, leaping, precise, to meet each melodious note as it rises from the orchestra pit. High we fly, on wings of fancy, and down to the edge of a wild forest, where begins . . .

The story of . . .

SWAN LAKE

PRINCE SIEGFRIED was celebrating his coming of age. Courtiers and peasants alike joined in the merry dancing, for the prince was not proud and chose his friends from all stations in life. The prince's tutor, Wolfgang, seemed not quite to have entered into the spirit of the party. He had entered too far into another kind of spirit, however, which quite went to his head and made him overbalance during the dance. This was more foolish than the antics of the Court Jester, and the prince laughed heartily to see his usually dignified tutor sprawled on the ground, legs kicking helplessly in the air. Wolfgang did not take the prince's teasing in good part, and made it clear that, in his opinion, the young man should be going about his business — that of ruling the Princedom — rather than mocking his tutor.

Despite their wish to be gay, a rather uneasy air had somehow descended on the group, which was not dispelled by the arrival of the prince's mother. She was not at all pleased to find her royal son mingling freely with the humble villagers, and reminded him sternly that he had an important duty to discharge the following night — namely to choose a bride at the Grand Ball.

The prince gloomily watched his mother sweep away towards the castle. The reminder of the Grand Ball had quite spoiled his birthday party. For Siegfried hoped to marry for love, and he loved none of the Court ladies from whom his mother wished him to choose a bride.

The revels continued, but the prince no longer took part in them. He wandered thoughtfully away by himself, gazing at the sky as if hoping to find the girl of his dreams up there among the clouds. Instead he saw passing overhead a flock of fine white swans, winging their way towards the setting sun. The young men of the group decided to go on a bird-hunting expedition, and armed with their bows, made for the lake. The others went off into the bushes in search of game, but Siegfried, feeling strangely sad and remote, preferred to stay by the lake looking over the water, which was calm and undisturbed as his own life had been until then. Yet suddenly the smooth surface of the lake shattered, cleaved by the bodies of white swans, who swam gracefully towards the bank where the prince stood. As they reached the verge, a distant clock struck midnight, and each swan unexpectedly turned into a lovely girl, dressed in downy white feathers. The leader of the group, wearing a crown, approached Siegfried, and begged him to spare their lives.

The swan girl was so beautiful that Siegfried could refuse her nothing. It appeared that her name was Queen Odette, who, with her hand-maidens, had been enchanted by a wicked magician. The girls were turned into swans and could only assume their own forms from midnight until dawn each day. And the spell was not to be broken until Odette had found a prince who would marry and love her for ever more. Siegfried had fallen in love with Odette the moment she had changed from being a swan into his dream girl. As for Odette, as soon as she started to dance with Prince Siegfried, on the banks of the lake, she knew that he was the only partner for her.

The prince had no sooner vowed to love Odette for ever, and asked her to be his wife, when the joyous moment was spoiled by the arrival of the wicked magician, disguised as an owl, who attacked Siegfried furiously. The prince refused to be daunted, however, and fought back so boldly that the magician went

fluttering owlishly away through the bushes. Siegfried's friends had heard the commotion, and came hurrying to see what was amiss. Mistaking the swan maidens for real swans they drew their bows, and Siegfried was only just able to stop them from releasing a volley of arrows at the defenseless creatures. Out of danger again, the swan maidens were so relieved that they performed a buoyant dance. Four of the youngest — they were no more than cygnets — made a pretty little group of their own, and Siegfried spent the hours until dawn arm in arm with his beloved Odette, watching the pleasant scene. When the light of day stole through the glade, all the maidens, and Odette too, turned back into swans and floated away down the lake out of sight. Siegfried returned to the palace in good cheer though, for he had arranged that Odette should come to the Grand Ball the following night, as soon as she had changed back into her own form. Naturally he intended to choose her as his bride, from among the other royal ladies who were to be invited. And once they were married Odette and her maidens could cast off their swan plumes for ever, since the wicked magician's spell would be broken.

The Ball was indeed a grand affair, attended by important guests from many countries, most of whom danced in their own particular national style. Great crystal chandeliers picked up colorful gleams of radiance from the ladies' precious jewels, and the gentlemen too wore their most splendid clothes. All the available princesses had been primped and powdered and bound and bustled, each hoping to be chosen to wed Prince Siegfried. Little did they guess that the prince had already made his choice, and was anxiously waiting until the stroke of midnight for Odette the Swan Queen to appear in her own exquisite shape. Long before that time, however, a

strange interruption took place. Into the ballroom, on the arm of a sinister looking man, came a young woman who resembled in all respects, the beautiful Odette herself. The likeness was so close, in fact, that Siegfried, quite forgetting that his beloved must still be swanlike until twelve o'clock, mistook the young woman for his queen. In fact the girl was really Odile, daughter of the wicked magician on whose arm she leaned. The magician had turned her, by dark enchantment, into the living image of Odette, so that the prince might be taken in. And so he was, utterly and completely. Siegfried had only danced once, from sheer politeness, with each princess in the room, but now he ran eagerly to the magician's daughter who he thought was Odette. Taking Odile in his arms he danced with her as if he would never let her go. The girl, deceitful as her father, was determined to become the prince's wife, and cunningly prevented him from glancing towards the window, where a white swan had appeared, beating its wings helplessly against the glass. The white swan was of course none other than Odette, the prince's true love, who was waiting desperately for midnight, in order to assume her real form. Still though, the hands of the clock had not reached twelve, and the unhappy bird was forced to watch Siegfried unknowingly promise himself to Odile, instead of to Odette. No sooner had the prince made his announcement than there came a deafening crash of thunder, which put out the lights and sent people screaming across the room. Only then did the prince see the frantic swan, who had been trying so hard all the time to attract his attention at the window. At last he realized that it was not yet midnight, and that the woman he had taken for his wife was not Odette by any means. The magician's plan had worked, and Siegfried had broken his vow of faithfulness to the Swan Queen. Now she and her maidens must remain swans for always.

With a cry of despair Siegfried ran from the room in pursuit of the Swan Queen, who, forsaken, had flown away through the stormy night. The prince hastened to the lake, anxious to explain the cruel trick that had been played upon him by the wicked magician. He found the weeping Odette, in her true form, for it was now past midnight, surrounded by her sorrowing maidens.

Odette forgave Siegfried instantly, but he had promised himself to another woman. Her heart, so full of love, had burst with anguish, and she could no longer live. When Siegfried discovered this he wanted to die too.

The wicked magician had followed the prince from the castle, ready to gloat upon the victim of his evil scheme. Siegfried, wild with anger and misery, fell upon the villain, and after a fearful struggle, hurled him bodily into the rising waters of the lake. The magician sank at once, dragged down by the black stone that was his heart, and met a just end.

Siegfried, seeing that Odette was dying, took her hand, and they too leaped into the lake. The waters closed gently over their heads as the serene glow of dawn touched the tips of the trees. The storm was over.

Odette's handmaidens were surprised to find that they had not changed back into swans with the coming of dawn. Looking towards the now tranquil lake, they saw a vision of Odette in all her radiant beauty, with Siegfried, the man who had loved her more than his own life. The handmaidens knew that the spell had at last been broken and that they were free. For in the end those who truly love can never be parted. Siegfried and Odette would stand together, in spirit, then and for always, by the quiet waters of Swan Lake.

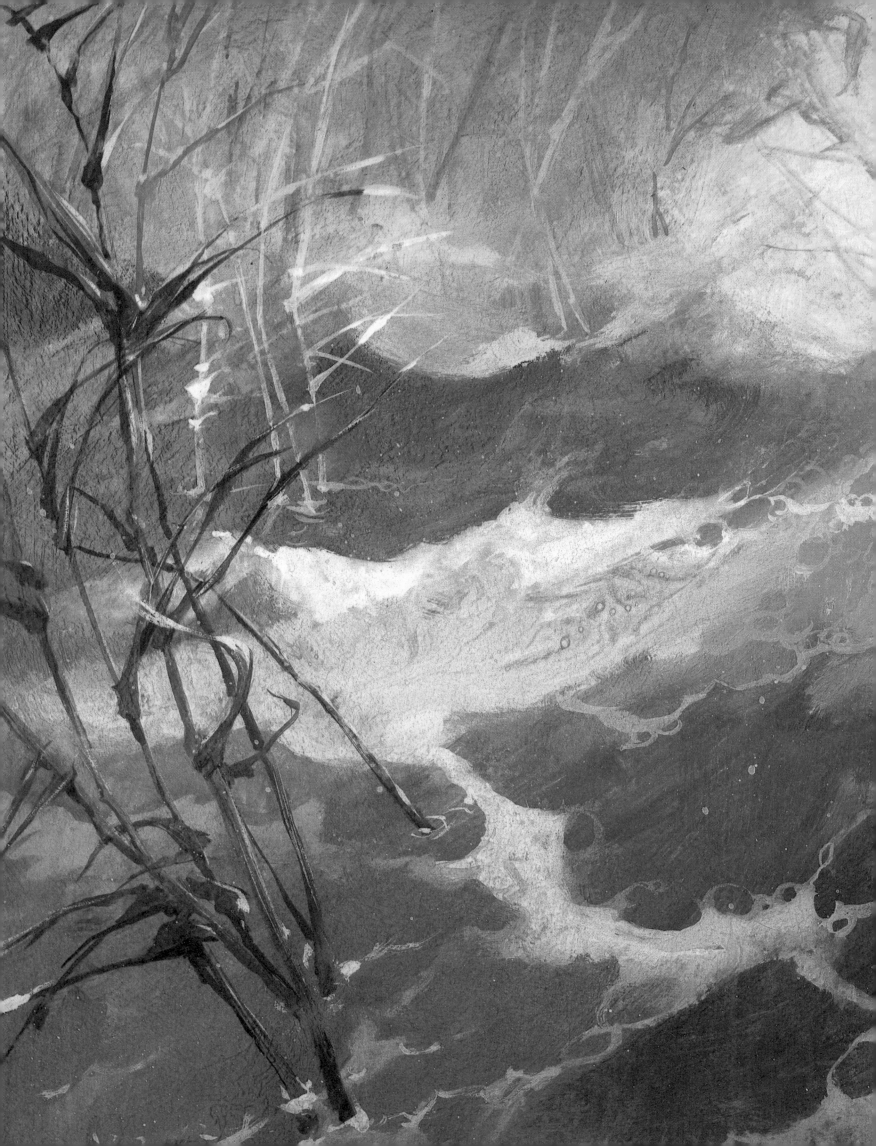

THE
SLEEPING
BEAUTY

THE TIME was any time but the present, and there was magic in the air. Part of the magic was a perfectly enchanting new baby, born to King Florestan and his wife. The small princess was to be called Aurora, and she lay in a golden cradle, waiting to be christened with that attractive name.

Of course there was to be a party, and Catalbutte, the Lord High Chamberlain, had sent out all the invitations. Or so he thought; but as is so often the case on these occasions, someone had been overlooked. And that someone was Carabosse, the wicked fairy, who was inclined to take exception in a most unpleasant way. Unaware of this, Catalbutte considered that he was handling the whole affair splendidly. Dressed in his finest clothes, and feeling extremely important, he unfurled a large scroll of parchment, ready to check each of the illustrious guests as they arrived. The king and queen, too, were wearing their best robes and crowns, and sat on State thrones, ready to welcome all the good fairies with their christening gifts for Princess Aurora.

Soon they began to arrive, by air or pumpkin coach as the fancy took them. Each fairy was escorted by two pages, carrying velvet cushions on which lay the presents. With low bows, they offered the royal child gifts of Beauty, Charm, Grace, Gentleness, Kindness and a thousand other virtues that Princess Aurora might well be glad of when she was old enough to appreciate them. The Lilac Fairy was delicate enough to contrive that the princess would always smell nice, while the Fairy of the Golden Vine made sure that Aurora would always have plenty of ripe grapes to eat. It seemed that the future of the baby princess was assured to perfection. At any rate she gurgled with evident satisfaction as the good fairies fluttered round the cradle, admiring her exquisite little top and toes and ribbons and bows. Lightly, so that their feet seemed hardly to touch the ground, the fairies performed a pretty dance before the king and queen, who smiled in graceful acknowledgment.

Suddenly, however, their smiles were dimmed by a dark cloud, seeping insidiously under the doors and through the windows of the throneroom. Ominous rolls of thunder made the walls — and those within them — shudder. A frightened page ran in and informed the king hoarsely that Carabosse was outside, demanding furiously why she had not been invited to the party.

The king went quite pale, whether with anger or fear no one could tell; but more than likely it was a little of each. Rushing to the chamberlain, he plucked the invitation list from Catalbutte's trembling hand. Sure enough there was no mention of Carabosse on the list, and the king dropped it in horror. The horror was in no way lessened, at this point, by the abrupt appearance of two

pairs of rats. The rats drew a black carriage, and inside was the wicked old witch, Carabosse. As twisted in form as she was in mind, the bad fairy swept out of her carriage towards the king, shaking her fist at him threateningly. It was clear she intended that the royal family should pay for their lack of hospitality. King Florestan explained that there had been an oversight, and that Catalbutte was to blame. The chamberlain, forgetting his pride, threw himself at the witch's feet, begging for mercy, and the malevolent old woman plucked off his wig and threw it scornfully to the ground. He was not even worthy of her disapproval. No, Carabosse intended that the king and queen should be made to suffer.

Darting to the cradle, the spiteful fairy announced that, though she had not been invited to the christening, still the baby princess should receive *her* gift too. No one could say that she, Carabosse, was ungenerous, whatever else they might happen to hold against her. Before it could be avoided, the horrid old creature had wished that Princess Aurora would one day prick her finger and die! With a wave of her black stick the spell was cast. Carabosse leaped exultantly back into her carriage and rode away on a flash of lightning, leaving the Court in deepest gloom.

The miserable cloud began to disperse, however, when the Lilac Fairy came forward to comfort the unhappy king and queen. She still had one more gift up her sleeve for Aurora. The princess, she promised, should not die when the wicked fairy's prophecy came about. Instead she would fall into a deep sleep, to be awakened only by the kiss of a handsome young prince.

The king, queen, courtiers and fairies encircled the cradle, hoping to surround the little princess with so much love that she would be safe from the evil intentions of Carabosse, the Black Fairy. And protect her they did, until one day some sixteen years later.

When Princess Aurora's sixteenth birthday occurred, the story of Carabosse and her cruel spell had been told so many times, and by so many different people, that some doubted it had ever really happened. The king and queen remembered the incident well enough though, but they kept the nasty thought tucked away in a drawer at the backs of their minds which was seldom opened.

Aurora herself knew nothing of the affair, for they had no wish to frighten her. Yet she did

sometimes wonder why pins and needles and all other sharp objects were so strictly banned from the palace by her father, the king. Only a while before her birthday party was to begin, Catalbutte, the chamberlain, had furiously ousted some black-clad old women who had been found engaged in the forbidden act of spinning.

There was to be a garden party, among the marble pillars and statues in the royal grounds, and the entrance of four princes from four parts of the world signalled the start of festivities. Wine flowed free as the fountain, but the princes took none. They were already intoxicated with delight at the sight of the beautiful Aurora, in her pink and silver brocade gown, and each was determined to win her for his wife before the evening was out. The princess's feet in their neat satin slippers pointed prettily, as she danced with the princes. She smiled provocatively at each of her suitors, and allowed them to whisper charming compliments in her delicate ears. But the

prince from Italy appealed to her no more than the prince from Spain. And the prince from England was no more successful in his proposal of marriage than the prince from India. How wonderful to be sixteen and sweet as lilac. Aurora wished at that moment she could remain so forever !

And as she wished, suddenly there appeared before the lovely young princess an aged crone, wearing a black hooded cloak. Aurora thought she must be one of the spinning ladies whom fussy old Catalbutte had sent away earlier. She was curious to know why the chamberlain had seemed so afraid of the spinners. This bent old creature certainly looked harmless enough. Indeed it appeared that the woman had a birthday present for Aurora, concealed in that heavy black cloak.

It was a golden spindle, and Aurora, who had never seen one before, accepted the gift with interest. Unaware of her danger, the gay princess began to waltz around, holding the gleaming spindle above her head. The king rose from his throne in horror, the queen screamed and everyone tried to take the spindle away from Aurora. It was too late though. The princess pricked her finger on the sharp point, faltered, and fell in a heavy trance. Not even a piercing shriek of triumph from the old crone — who was none other than the wicked Carabosse — could waken Aurora.

Carabosse took herself off in a huff and a puff of smoke, leaving the king in a rage, the queen in tears, and the rest of the Court in a state of utter confusion. The four princes saw that the party was well and truly over. Lifting the still body of Aurora they placed it gently on a silken couch, and went home sadly to their respective countries.

It was then that the Lilac Fairy appeared, cool and collected as ever she had been sixteen years before. Waving her wand, she caused everyone there to join the princess in her timeless sleep.

At once the king stopped raging, the queen stopped weeping, and the courtiers ceased to fret.

Dreamily they all settled themselves comfortably on the grass, as if it had been a great green quilted bed, and were soon dead to the world.

Years passed — a hundred of them to be exact — and still they slept on, while the castle crumbled and creepers crept and tiny acorns grew to forest oaks. Fashions had changed, yet a peasant was still a peasant, and a prince was still a prince.

And of the princes there was none more handsome in all the land than young Prince Florimund, as he strode, clad in red from cap to boots, at the head of his hunting party. Gallison, the royal tutor, was exhausted by the chase, and suggested that the group should now devote themselves to a more decorous occupation, such as blindman's buff. The nobles agreed, provided Gallison would play blind man, but they led him such a dance that he was soon glad to go off hunting with them again.

Florimund would have joined his friends had he not been compelled, by some strange means, to stay where he was. Twining roots curled round his feet to detain him, while the thick, scented branches of the trees closed inwards to bar his way. Florimund felt suddenly light-headed and dreamy; and as in a dream, a wide lake appeared before him. On the lake, in a mother-of-pearl boat, sailed the Lilac Fairy, her wand upraised. As the boat came to land the Fairy stepped out and touched the prince with the tip of the wand. Faint and cloudy, there appeared to Florimund an entrancing vision of the Sleeping Princess. It seemed to him that the lovely girl might wake if only he could touch her. But try as he would, the spirit of Aurora floated tantalizingly just out of reach. A deep longing gripped Florimund to rouse that still spirit with the warmth of his love; to breathe into her coldly marbled form the energy of life. If she did truly exist, he begged the

Lilac Fairy to lead him to this girl of his desire.

The Lilac Fairy held out her hand and drew Prince Florimund into the magic boat. Music rose high from the enchanted forest, like a wind, swelling the gossamer sails, and bearing the boat on down the lake to where time stood still.

On the other side of the lake was an old castle, and Florimund was shocked to see two sentries fast asleep at their posts. His disapproval did not rouse them, however, and wandering further, the prince came across the recumbent forms of King Florestan and his Court, as unchanged as when they had laid themselves down to sleep a hundred years before. The Lilac Fairy led him to a silken couch, over which spiders had thoughtfully woven a gauze web to protect the Sleeping Princess. Prince Florimund pulled the web apart, leaned over and saw Aurora, more beautiful in reality than she had appeared in his vision. Swiftly he bent and kissed her delicate face. Aurora's long lashes fluttered and raised to reveal her eyes, dark and clear as the lake on which Florimund had sailed to his true love. And Aurora, looking at Florimund, saw her true love in him.

Now that the bad spell was broken at last, the palace and the gardens became exactly as they had been a century before. King Florestan sat up and stretched, as though he had merely dozed off for five minutes, instead of a hundred years. The queen and her ladies were putting their hair to rights, while the Lord Chamberlain, concerned as ever for his appearance, consulted a mirror and was gratified to find that he had not changed in the least.

As soon as Prince Florimund had asked, and been granted, the hand of Princess Aurora, the king decided that enough time had been wasted already, and that the wedding should take place at once.

It was a fairy tale affair, and all the fairy folk were there. Puss-in-Boots escorted, with his usual gallantry, the White Cat. Little Red Riding Hood came with the Wolf, who was on his best behavior, and ate nothing but cake. Prince Charming and Cinderella, in her glass slippers, arrived with Hop-o'-my-Thumb astride the Blue Bird.

What rejoicing there was that night! Aurora the bride, dressed all in white, could have danced with her prince for a hundred years more, so full of love and life was she. The Sleeping Princess, who had slept so long, was awake at last.

GISELLE

ALBRECHT, the young Duke of Silesia, strode through a woodland glade, followed somewhat doubtfully by his attendant, Wilfrid. The duke's manner was noble enough, but his clothes might have belonged to the simplest peasant — as indeed they had until Wilfrid borrowed them. The fact was that Albrecht had disguised himself, in order to visit a young woman of the village, whose charm had attracted his attention. The young woman was called Giselle, and she was not accustomed to dukes.

Being the prettiest girl in those parts, Giselle had many other admirers, including Hilarion the gamekeeper, and it was generally considered that he, of all the peasant lads, had the best chance of winning her hand. That was until she met Albrecht, of course. He introduced himself as Loys,

a humble woodsman, who lived in a hut nearby, and from that moment Giselle had no eyes for any other man, not even for Hilarion, who came upon the scene and found the disguised duke and Giselle looking at each other lovingly. This did not please Hilarion, and he told the so-called Loys to be off. The duke was not used to being addressed in such a manner, and nearly informed the fellow to whom he was speaking. However, remembering that Giselle might be frightened and overawed to find herself in the presence of a nobleman, he continued to play his part of woodsman. Hilarion went off in disgust, for it was clear that Giselle no longer welcomed his presence.

Giselle began to dance lightheartedly with Albrecht, and they were joined by some vinepickers, passing through the glade with their baskets. Berthe, Giselle's mother, came upon them and admonished her daughter for this display of abandoned gaiety. Berthe felt that no good would come of Giselle's passion for dancing, for that region was said to be haunted by the ghosts of maidens who had been too fond of dancing. These maidens — they were called Wilis — had all died disappointed in love, and were said to appear in the early hours of the morning, to seek

revenge on their unfaithful lovers. Berthe was afraid that unless Giselle began to take life more seriously, she would lose it altogether, and end up as one of the unhappy Wilis. But Giselle would not heed her mother's warning, and danced on without a care.

The sound of a hunting horn was heard, and the vinepickers remembered that they still had

work to do. Taking up their baskets, they went on into the forest, followed by Loys. Giselle accompanied her mother back to their home, which stood near an empty cottage. It was there that the Duke of Silesia would change into his peasant dress and assume the identity of Loys, so that he could court the beautiful Giselle. Along came Hilarion, sullen to be rejected so unexpectedly by his sweetheart, and seeing that the glade was, for the moment, deserted, he darted into Loy's cottage, intent on mischief.

The hunting party now arrived, led by the Prince of Courland and his daughter, Princess Bathilde. Berthe, honored to be of service to the royal group, offered refreshments which they were pleased to accept. Princess Bathilde so far forgot her lofty position as to speak in quite a friendly way to Giselle, who soon lost her shyness and talked quite merrily of her simple life in the forest, and of how she loved to dance. She even confided in the princess about her handsome young suitor, Loys, and Bathilde listened with an indulgence she would not have felt had she known that the Loys of whom Giselle spoke was really her own fiancé, the Duke of Silesia himself, to whom she had been betrothed since childhood. In fact Giselle's story and the little dance she did to illustrate it (in spite of her mother's disapproving glance) delighted the princess, who gave Giselle a golden chain for having so greatly diverted her.

The Prince of Courland was not as young as he had been, and asked that he might be allowed

to rest for a while in Berthe's cottage before continuing the hunt. He and the princess went inside, as the vinepickers returned heavily laden to the glade. Loys was with them, and he and Giselle embraced warmly. Hilarion, in the doorway of Loys' cottage, saw them and was consumed with jealousy. He had found the fine garments and belongings of the Duke of Silesia, and guessed that Loys was an impostor. Dashing to Giselle, Hilarion proffered a crested sword and an embroidered cloak, as proof that she had been deceived, and that her lover was no peasant but a nobleman of the bluest blood. Giselle could not bring herself to believe this, and Hilarion, beside himself with chagrin, plucked a hunting horn from Loys' belt and sounded a sharp blast, which brought the prince and princess out of Berthe's cottage.

Of course the Prince of Courland and his daughter instantly recognized Loys, despite his peasant dress, as Duke Albrecht, and now Giselle was forced to accept the truth. It was clear that the man she loved could never belong to her. He was born to a higher station in life, and must marry the Princess Bathilde to whom he had been engaged. This was too much for Giselle to bear, and she went quite out of her mind with shock. Her limbs seemed no longer to obey her, but moved with a strange unnatural will of their own, in a sorrowful dance back along the paths of yesterday, when she and Loys had loved and been happy. Her movements became more and more frenzied as she acted again each precious moment of the time they had spent together, until at last the agony of the present was upon her. Seizing the duke's sword from Hilarion, Giselle stabbed herself to the heart, before any of the horrified onlookers could prevent her.

It was a sad group around Berthe, who hugged the body of her child as if she would keep the life in it by force. But the soul of Giselle had already fled to the inmost depths of the forest, where the Wilis danced by the light of dawn.

Time passed, and Hilarion, recovered from the grief and guilt he had felt after Giselle's death, went out hunting one night with some companions. They came by chance upon a small clearing in the forest, where stood a marble grave. The white light of the moon, filtering through the tangled branches, showed clearly the name 'Giselle' etched on the stone. Hilarion would have stayed there a while with his memories, but a church clock chiming midnight struck a cold chill in the bones of the others, and they persuaded him away.

Only just in time, for the glade was suddenly peopled with the flitting ghostly figures of the Wilis, those maidens who had died unlucky in love. They stretched out their tapered fingers as if seeking to drag the young men who had wronged them to their doom. The Queen of the Wilis, Myrta, stood among them, and like a breeze, without substance, she moved towards the grave of Giselle. Waving her wand, which was a sprig of rosemary, Myrta commanded the spirit of Giselle to rise and join the Wilis in their mournful dance. From out of the grave came the

white lovely form of Giselle, who had laid so still, but now danced once again as vivaciously as she had in life.

Hilarion, lured by some inexplainable urge, had left his friends and returned to Giselle's grave. Now the Wilis were all about him, flinging themselves wildly into a dance which Hilarion found himself obliged to join. Back and forth stepped the Wilis in hectic motion, sweeping Hilarion with them, until reeling with exhaustion he fell into a nearby lake and was drowned. The Wilis had taken vengeance again that night.

To this cold and haunted place came Albrecht with his loyal retainer Wilfrid, to see where Giselle had been laid to rest. The young duke had been full of remorse for his deception, and blamed himself for causing Giselle's death. Wilfrid, sensing though not seeing the restless shades, begged his master to come away. But Albrecht had caught a fleeting glimpse of a sprite who darted between the trees, light and graceful as only Giselle could be. He motioned Wilfrid to depart, and advanced eagerly in the direction of the flying figure. The Wilis came towards him, ready to lead yet another victim in a dance of death. However, Myrta, their Queen, ordered them to stand back. It was for Giselle, the newest Wili, to dance this young man to his doom, for it was he who had misused her.

Giselle, who still loved Albrecht in spirit, refused to harm him. So that he might be safe from the evil magic of the queen, she told him to cling to the cross on her grave. Albrecht did so, and the queen, angry to find that she was unable to enchant him while he was under the protection of the cross, ordered Giselle to lure him from it. Despite her desire to save Albrecht, Giselle had become a Wili, and was fated, like the others, to obey the queen. Her reluctant feet began to move in compliance with the queen's command, and Albrecht felt drawn by an irresistible force towards her. Tearing himself away from the cross, he and Giselle were soon engaged in a mad whirl. Faster and faster they went, joined exultantly by the other Wilis; and though Albrecht felt his strength ebbing, he was unable to stop.

The young duke would surely have died from exhaustion if the church clock had not at last sounded the hour of four. It was time for the Wilis to return to their resting places, and one by one they slowly faded from view, until only Giselle remained.

In vain Albrecht, gasping painfully for breath, tried to hold on to his beloved. But Giselle too had to go back to her white marble grave, and as Albrecht watched agonized, she vanished. His life was saved, yet it stretched before him empty and meaningless. For he had lost Giselle, who had danced away with his heart, forever.

THE
NUTCRACKER

CHRISTMAS EVE, and everyone wearing his party best; even the tree shimmered and showed off its finery, for the Head Town Councilor had invited some guests to dine. Yet it was the children's season, and the party was really for Fritz and Clara. They and their friends scampered about gleefully, trying hard to undo the effects of mother's careful grooming.

In came old Councilor Drosselmayer, a somewhat sharp, birdlike gentleman who was to play the part of Santa Claus. At once order was restored — out of respect for the parcels he carried, as much as for anything. Fritz and Clara wanted to see what their Uncle Drosselmayer had brought them, even before the other children had been given their presents. To teach them better manners, they were handed a pie and a cabbage, amid laughter in which the greedy ones were too shamefaced to join. They were merrier in a moment, however, for Drosselmayer, taking the pie from Fritz, lifted the lid and out popped a fine clockwork soldier! And Clara's cabbage actually

contained a pretty doll. When the toys were wound, they performed a lively dance, to the equal delight of the young and not-so-young.

When all the gifts had been opened and appreciated, the word "bed" was mentioned, and of course the children suddenly became hard of hearing. The word was spoken again, this time so loudly, and by so many parents, that most of the young guests began to take their gloves, cloaks and farewells.

44

Clara, who was a year younger than Fritz, and still thought that good times lasted for ever, became tearful. To send her upstairs more cheerfully, kind old Drosselmayer found one more gift in a corner of his sack. It was a nutcracker, made in the shape of a soldier standing hard to attention. Quite pacified, Clara danced around, bidding everyone good-night and showing off her new toy. Fritz, in fact, considered that she was showing off far too much for a young sister, and snatched the nutcracker away. Clara stamped her foot crossly and demanded the return of the toy, but Fritz, who really should have been wiser as well as older, threw the nutcracker across the floor. That was the end of the nutcracker, for the time being at any rate, and the end of Clara and Fritz too, for they were dispatched bedwards without more delay.

The grown-ups were left to continue the party on a more dignified note, but at last it was even their bedtime, and they all went home. The Head Councilor and his wife put out the lights and retired, leaving the candles on the Christmas tree palely glowing in the still and shadowy room.

A small figure stole cautiously round the door. It was Clara, who had come to retrieve the fallen nutcracker. In the flickering haze, the room looked quite different somehow. The chairs, tables and pictures seemed no longer to be the solid reliable objects that Clara had

always thought them, but had taken on a blur-edged, dreamy quality. And when the cuckoo came out of the clock to strike midnight, did not that sharp-eyed bird resemble her Uncle Drosselmayer to a most extraordinary degree? Clara began to feel not quite comfortable, and hastened to find the nutcracker so that she could be off safely to bed, like the good little girl she was always trying to be. There the nutcracker was, on the floor where Fritz had, so infuriatingly, flung it. Clara was about to pick up the nutcracker when she heard a skittling and a scuttling from the woodwork.

Mice! thought Clara, and jumped on a chair in alarm. But she need not have been afraid, for the mice were far too busy to pay her the slightest attention. They were actually engaged in a furious battle beneath the Christmas tree with an army of tin soldiers, led, quite astonishingly, by the nutcracker soldier himself! The mice were winning the battle tails down, for they outnumbered the soldiers four to one. Clara, from her discreet position on the chair, cried encouragement, but gallantly though he fought, the nutcracker was almost downed by the king mouse. In her anxiety to help, Clara threw caution to the winds — and her shoe at the enemy. Seeing their leader fall, the other mice retired in confusion to the trenches in the woodwork, leaving the nutcracker's army victorious. The victor approached and made Clara a deep bow. But to her amazement, when he straightened up the nutcracker had turned into a live soldier prince. As a

reward for saving his life, the prince offered to take Clara back to his kingdom on the Shore of Sweets; and Clara, now that she had recovered from her misgivings, was not slow to accept.

The frosted-cotton balls on the Christmas tree suddenly turned into swirling white snow-flakes, settling softly on Clara's eyelids so that they closed. When she could see again, the walls and ceiling of the room had vanished. Neither was the carpet beneath her feet the old familiar one which was becoming a little worn round the fireplace — for Clara now stood on a carpet of thick snow. There were white-capped trees in the distance, but her very own Christmas tree was still there, its gentle light giving out kindly warmth. The soldier prince stood by her side reassuringly, as a band of gnomes marched by, heralding the arrival of the Snow King and Queen, through whose land they must pass to reach the Shore of Sweets. Their majesties, wearing icicle crowns, greeted Clara coolly but regally, and they performed a stately waltz, in company with their subjects, the gnomes, to entertain the visitor.

Clara was enchanted in more ways than one, and when some of the snowflakes gathered to-gether, at the king's command, into a magic sleigh, she stepped blithely in beside the prince, and slid off down a frozen river towards the Shore of Sweets.

The journey seemed to take no time at all, for Clara hardly blinked once before she found herself clambering out of the sleigh on to a rock of candy. Waiting to greet them was the

Sugarplum Fairy, a lovely lady in a tasteful outfit of pink spun-sugar.

The Sugarplum Fairy, preceded by twelve young pages armed with lanterns, led the way into the royal palace. There, seated on a throne which was studded with all kind and color of sweets imaginable, the nutcracker prince told how Clara had saved his life in the battle with the mouse king. The Sugarplum Fairy announced that a huge banquet should be held in honor of the heroine. Then Clara, for once, was able to eat her fill of chocolate cream bars, for there was a different flavor to each course.

Afterwards a ball was held on a polished toffee floor, and a chocolate-shaded Turk performed a delightful dance. After the entertainment, the prince himself rose to choose his partner for the final waltz. Clara was afraid he might ask the Sugarplum Fairy, who was certainly a very fine dancer, for she too had given a splendid display that evening. But he offered his arm to the Guest of Honor, and honored indeed was Clara to dance with the handsome nutcracker prince.

As the last strains of the waltz were played, Clara began to grow very sleepy. The buzzing of a thousand bees hummed in her ears. She felt as if she were sinking down into a soft sea of honey that closed above her head, shutting out all sight and sound . . . .

Clara awoke in her own bed at home, and with only a nutcracker, lying downstairs beneath the tree where Fritz had thrown it, to remind her of a very sweet dream.

PETRUSHKA

EVERYONE in St. Petersburg had come to the fair in Admiralty Square, for it was the season of Shrove-Tide and general revelry. Lustily barkers exhorted the crowds to Walk Up and Witness the Wonders of the World at their sidestalls. Gaily, if discordantly, the barrel organs ground away to muffled accompaniment of numberless shifting feet.

A sharp rat-tattle on the drums announced that a show was about to begin. In front of a small theater appeared the Charlatan — a sinister looking fellow in a tall pointed hat and robes marked with queer symbols. The Charlatan was by trade a puppeteer. But by nature he was an arrant trickster, and dabbled more than he should in the dangerous art of magic.

That day the Charlatan pronounced himself the greatest puppet-master on earth. For he claimed to have given his wooden dolls life itself! An incredulous murmur arose from the spectators as the Charlatan pulled back the curtains of the small theater. Three puppets were revealed; Petrushka, the Blackamoor and the Ballerina, propped stiff as three bundles of firewood. The audience jeered derisively and called out that the show had better become more lively or they would transfer their attention elsewhere. The Charlatan, however, was unabashed. Deftly he drew from his wide sleeve a flute, and sounded three sharp notes. To everyone's amazement

the three puppets at once pulled themselves together, threw off their strings and jerked unaided into a dance. Now the crowd stamped and clapped their approval, then settled down to watch in fascination as the splendid Blackamoor in his glittering costume, and the pathetic pale clown Petrushka, vied for the attention of the beautiful Ballerina, whom they both loved passionately.

It was clear that the Blackamoor, with his vigorous movements and glossy white-paint smile, was favored by the flirtatious Ballerina. But it was Petrushka, a figure of fun in his baggy clothes, moving clumsily and to ill-effect, who loved her deeply. For though the other two puppets had magically come alive at the Charlatan's command, Petrushka was the only one with real feeling.

Seeing that his rival was getting the better of him, poor Petrushka so far forgot himself and his audience as to leap out among them, in furious pursuit of the Blackamoor. The Charlatan was obliged to catch the puppets and return them hastily to their quarters, for, having been released from their strings and given wills of their own, they were quite out of control.

Petrushka, whom the Charlatan blamed for spoiling the show, was thrown roughly into his room, and he lay where he had fallen, wooden limbs all askew, too despairing to move. How

much happier he had been before the Charlatan, with his interfering magic, had brought him to life. Now he could feel and suffer, when before he had been hard and unmoved as the trunk of the tree from which he was hewn. Nobody cared for Petrushka. The Charlatan was cruel and had only created him for his own benefit. The Blackamoor, who was proud and vain, despised him. And as for the Ballerina whom he adored more than his enchanted life, she cared for none

but her pretty self, and soon made it clear. For the door opened and in she tripped, a frivolous little creature, delighting in her conquest, even if it was only of shabby Petrushka.

Petrushka, with new hope at the sight of her, sprang up and began to dance about comically, twisting and turning smartly in the air and doing all kinds of clever acrobatics, in the hope of making a good impression. But the Ballerina had come to *be* admired, not to admire, and ran out pettishly leaving Petrushka more crestfallen than ever.

Ashamed and angry at his failure, he charged about the room, striking his wooden body against the walls as though to break himself apart. But it was only his heart that broke.

Meanwhile in the adjoining room, which was sumptuously decorated with Eastern silks and treasures, the Moor lay idly toying with a coconut. Wondering what it contained, the savage fellow took a curved sword from the wall, and struck downwards. The nut was a tough one though, and would not be split. So the Moor touched his wooden head to the floor, in pagan respect for the coconut's endurance!

Just then the Ballerina peeped round the door, and seeing herself more than welcome, came darting in. She pirouetted round the Moor and soon they were both waltzing about together, conceited as a pair of peacocks, trying to outdo each other in grace and movement.

Next door miserable Petrushka heard them, and in an excess of rage he began again hammering himself against the wall. Such was his determined onslaught that the wall actually gave way, and Petrushka shot into the room and sat up in a pile of rubble. He looked so absurd that the Moor and the Ballerina leaned against each other, laughing helplessly. Petrushka sprang up, reckless with humiliation, and flung himself at the Moor. The Ballerina showed then how little she cared

for either of them, by fainting carefully in a corner, as far away from the battle as possible.

Gamely Petrushka fought and with such frenzy that he might even have beaten the strong and powerful Moor in fair contest. But the Moor stooped and picked up his curved sword. Sweeping it in a wide arc over his head, he chased the defenseless Petrushka out of the room, through the front of the theater and out into the square.

The fair was still in full swing, and a performing bear, plodding heavily obedient to the piper's tune, now attracted the crowd. A tipsy merchant staggered about foolishly, giving away his money, and as the notes fluttered out of his hands, everyone nearby pushed and scrambled and trampled one upon the other to get some. For money was not often found flying loose in St. Petersburg. Masqueraders cavorted, disguised as goats and pigs, teased by the trident of a painted devil in horns and forked tail.

Into this bizarre gathering ran Petrushka, and he ran for his life. The Moor was close behind, his sword upraised, and the bear and the merchant and the devil himself lost their appeal. The crowds stood grimly watching as the Moor gained swiftly on Petrushka and swept down his sword. Presently all that remained of Petrushka, and his love for the Ballerina, was a heap of chopped wood. And the Moor crept away to hide in shame.

The frolicsome noise of the fair died to horrified silence. Someone brought the Charlatan to see the result of his meddling magic, and so indignant were the spectators that they closed in on him threateningly. The Charlatan cowered, protesting that he was not to blame for the tragedy. In truth, he whined, the puppets were nothing more than ordinary blocks of wood, and of no account whatever. Doubtfully the crowd looked down at the splintered remains of Petrushka. Perhaps indeed they were wasting their sympathy on a doll, made not of flesh and blood but of wood and sawdust. Gradually they dispersed, muttering among themselves, but leaving the Charlatan unharmed.

Alone and safe, the wizard shed no tears of sorrow over the fate of Petrushka. Instead he dragged what was left of the unfortunate doll back towards the theater — intending no doubt to enjoy his supper before a cheerfully blazing hearth. But as he neared the booth, the Charlatan stood back and shook in terror. For there on the roof above, bathed in cold white light, was the ghostly form of Petrushka, pointing a stark wood finger accusingly and crying out against him.

Petrushka's life, which the Charlatan had so thoughtlessly given, had been destroyed. But his soul, which was born of love, would live on to haunt the magician until the day he died.

COPPELIA

IN THE QUAINT old town of Galicia there lived a quaint old gentleman called Coppelius. Coppelius was a toymaker, and he had made a doll which was lifelike enough to have been his own daughter. Indeed he named the doll Coppelia, after himself, and enjoyed pretending she was really human. He would set Coppelia up at the window, her glazed enamel-blue eyes staring ahead dreamlessly, and watch the reaction of passing folk, who were plainly taken in by her natural

appearance. One young man, Franz, was so far taken in, in fact, as to quite lose his foolish head over the beautiful doll, much to the annoyance of his true lady-love, Swanilda.

Franz was always making some excuse to pass by the toymaker's house, in the hope of seeing the mysterious lady at the window, and once the mischievous Coppelius hid behind the doll and lifted her arm up and down, so that Franz, thinking she waved encouragement, blew her a gale of kisses. Swanilda saw from the window of her own room across the street, and the next time Franz asked her to join the dance with him in the village square, she refused. Franz was crestfallen, for deep down inside he was extremely fond of Swanilda. To prove it he asked her, then and there, to be his wife.

Swanilda had no time to reply to Franz's proposal, for the burgomaster arrived with a proclamation to read. It appeared that the lord of the manor was to present the village with a new bell for the clock tower, and that a fête was to be held the following day, in celebration. Furthermore,

said the burgomaster, whoever married on that day would receive a fine present from the lord. For festival time was the time to wed in that village.

The villagers cheered delightedly, and certain young men approached certain young women with the same question that Franz had asked Swanilda. But Swanilda herself picked up a whispering sheaf of corn and held it to her ear, and the corn whispered that Franz did not yet love her truly. Whereupon Swanilda turned down his proposal and chose another partner to dance with, so that Franz should see how little she cared.

Franz was so put out that he decided to favor only Coppelia with his affection from then onwards. He was determined that night to confront her at last, and ask for her hand in marriage. Perhaps then Swanilda might regret the chance she had missed of catching a fine husband!

Towards evening old Coppelius decided to stretch his spindly legs in a walk around the village square. Carefully he locked his front door with a large key and tottered off, straight into the midst of a mob of pranksters, who had started celebrating the fête even before it had begun. Testily the toymaker held out his cane to hold them off, but the irritating fellows snatched it out of his hand and obliged the old gentleman to career about with them in a most undignified manner. The encounter neither improved his balance nor his temper, and when the tormentors had danced away to find another victim, Coppelius departed outraged, without noticing that he had dropped his key.

Soon afterwards Swanilda and her friends happened to come along. Seeing the key, Swanilda discovered that it fitted the lock of the toymaker's door. Here at last was a chance to confront Coppelia, and perhaps learn the secret of her rival's charm! The others followed Swanilda into the house, just as eager to satisfy their curiosity, and they all trooped into the toymaker's workshop.

In the meager light that filtered through the latticed windows, the girls were startled at first to make out a collection of people, sprawled grotesquely here and there on the floor or across the benches. Someone screamed, having bumped into the still figure of a Chinese gentleman in silken robes who suddenly began to move forward menacingly. The girls would have run away there and then but for Swanilda, who found that the Chinaman and all the other figures were only great stuffed clockwork dolls.

Delightedly now, everyone began to wind the keys in the backs of the toys, and the mechanical creatures all started to dance. Crusader partnered Harlequin in his diamond patches, while Pierrot swept a sharp-capped Astronomer round the workshop, in perfect time. The dolls whirled on as long as their clockwork springs would let them, and then fell together in an untidy heap.

Swanilda was looking for Coppelia meanwhile, and found her behind a curtained alcove. Coppelia sat, ladylike as ever, looking unblinkingly back at Swanilda.

Not a word did she reply to Swanilda's polite, if chilly greeting, and even when prodded showed no sign of retaliation. Suddenly Swanilda saw that Coppelia was no more real than any of the other toys in the workshop. Her silly Franz had fallen in love with a pretty doll! Now he

should be cured of his fickleness once and for all. Drawing the curtain behind her, Swanilda stripped the superior Coppelia of her fine clothes and changed into them herself.

The girls were having such splendid fun in the toymaker's workshop that they quite forgot Coppelius might return, until all at once there he was, standing in the doorway and shaking his fist angrily at them. Startled they fled from the house, sharply propelled by the toymaker's

cane. Only Swanilda was left, and she was hidden behind the curtain disguised as Coppelia the doll.

The old man fussed about, propping his toys back in their correct positions, and once he even looked to see if Coppelia was undamaged. She seemed much the same as ever, his precious doll, and Coppelius sank down, relieved, on his bench. A moment later, however, he sprang up indignantly, for a window had opened and a face appeared in its frame. The face was followed by the head, shoulders and the rest of Franz, who had climbed up the side of the house by ladder to pay his respects to Coppelia. With a great effort the toymaker controlled his fury, and somewhat to Franz's surprise, welcomed him quite cordially. In fact old Coppelius thought he would attempt an experiment on this interloper, who deserved to be taught a lesson. He would try to transfer the life force of this impertinent scoundrel to Coppelia. Then at last the toymaker could boast of a real daughter, warm and laughing as any girl, to make him feel young again.

Franz, hardly expecting to be received so kindly by Coppelius, nevertheless settled himself down and accepted a glass of wine. He had hoped to find the toymaker away from home, but since this was not the case, he thought he might as well make the best of the situation. After the wine, which would no doubt give him the courage to speak plainly, he would make an offer for the hand of Coppelia, man to man and no nonsense. But the more wine Franz drank, the more difficult it was to speak plainly, or indeed to speak at all. Soon he was snoring soundly, for the toymaker had put a strong sleeping draught in the drink.

All this was seen by Swanilda from behind the curtain where she hid, dressed as Coppelia. Now she watched as the toymaker pored eagerly over some learned books, hoping to find out how to give Franz's life to the doll. But none of the books was learned enough to explain this. However, Coppelius had studied a little magic in his youth, and decided to try one or two spells of his own. He drew the curtain across the alcove, and there sat Swanilda, quite still and staring blankly ahead, exactly like Coppelia. The old man, with his failing eyesight, was completely deceived. Mumbling some strange enchantment, and waving his arms absurdly, Coppelius sought to turn his toy into a real person. Swanilda soon realized what he was about, and, instead of punishing Franz, she now decided to pay Coppelius out for trying to harm him. She still loved Franz, you see, in spite of his faults.

Moving her limbs in jerky imitation of a doll, Swanilda rose and started solemnly to dance round the toymaker. Coppelius began to think himself a good deal more clever than he actually was, for it appeared his enchantment had worked. There was Coppelia, as she moved and breathed, a girl of the most genuine variety! He, the toymaker of Galicia, had managed to make a living doll, and now she should obey his every command.

Swanilda entered spiritedly into the game, pretending to bow to the old man's will. When he

threw on her shoulders a black mantilla, she flung into a passionate Spanish bolero. When Coppe-lius, delighted, put on her a plaid shawl, she promptly executed a smart Scottish reel. The toy-maker's rapture was cut short, however, by a sudden change of mood on the part of the human doll. The sight of poor stupified Franz, lying helpless in his chair, made Swanilda furious. She ran about, shaking the stuffing from dolls, kicking the furniture and tearing pages from the magic book. Coppelius backed in alarm. It seemed that he had, unaccountably, lost control of his marvelous doll. He now began to regret having, as he thought, given her life, if this was to be the way she intended to lead it.

Swanilda took Franz by the shoulders and shook him into wakefulness. Then, before the startled toymaker could stop them, she dragged her drowsy lover to the window, and down the ladder, towards his home.

Hurrying to the alcove, Coppelius searched behind the chair and found the wooden body of Coppelia, stripped of her finery, lying lifeless as ever, on the floor. Thoroughly frightened and upset, as he most certainly deserved to be, the old man collapsed heavily amid the ruins of his workshop.

When Franz learned that he had forsaken the warm and lively Swanilda for a stupid sawdust

doll, he was truly ashamed of himself. The following morning, when the fête had begun, he humbly apologized and asked Swanilda once more to be his wife. This time, knowing that she would never again have a rival, Swanilda agreed.

It was a happy day. The lord of the manor had given his bell for the clock tower, and his blessing to the young couples who were to be married. Among them were Franz and Swanilda, dazzled with the joy they had newly found in each other.

Even old Coppelius, having recovered from the shock of yesterday's disturbance, came to the fête, telling his misfortune to all who would listen. He complained so loudly and bitterly that even the lord of the manor heard him. Swanilda was sent for, and contrite now, she offered to pay her wedding dowry to Coppelius, in compensation for the damage she had caused. But the lord of the manor was a generous man, and gave the old toymaker some gold instead, which put him in a better frame of mind than even a real live daughter could have!

The new bell in the church tower rang out sweetly that evening. It rang for the wedding of Franz and Swanilda, who danced until dawn. And from then onwards they never changed partners again.

74

Notes on the Ballets

SWAN LAKE *was first performed in* 1877 *at the Bolshoi Theater in Moscow. The music for this popular ballet was written by the famed Russian composer Peter Ilich Tchaikovsky.*

THE SLEEPING BEAUTY, *one of the most popular ballets performed today, is based on the familiar fairy tale by Charles Perrault. Peter Ilich Tchaikovsky also composed the music for this ballet.*

GISELLE, *with music by Adolphe Adam, was first performed in* 1841 *in Paris. The role of Giselle is one of the most difficult in ballet, for it requires the leading ballerina to be both an excellent dancer and an excellent actress.*

THE NUTCRACKER, *another ballet with music by Peter Ilich Tchaikovsky, has become a traditional Christmas entertainment in many places. It is a favorite ballet for children.*

PETRUSHKA *is performed to the lively music by Igor Stravinsky. One of many ballets depicting dolls that come to life, "Petrushka" was first performed in Paris in* 1911.

COPPELIA *is also known as the ballet of "The Girl With the Enamel Eyes". The music for this ballet, which was first performed in* 1870, *was composed by Leo Delibes.*

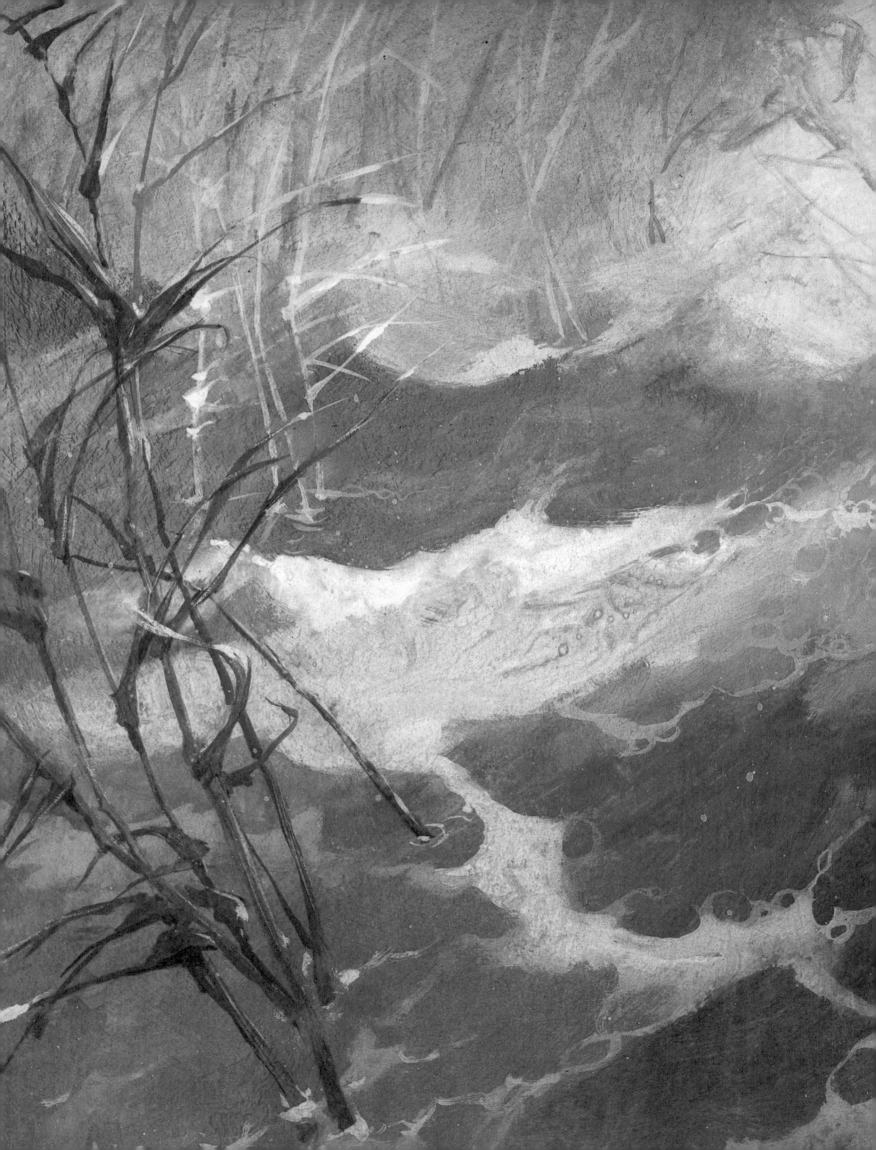